LIVING

BY THE SCRIPT

*Making the Most
of Your Life*

DEJI AJIBADE

First published in Great Britain as a softback original in 2021

Copyright © Deji Ajibade

The moral right of this author has been asserted.

All rights reserved.

No part of this publication may be reproduced, stored in a retrieval system, or transmitted, in any form or by any means, without the prior permission in writing of the author, nor be otherwise circulated in any form of binding or cover other than that in which it is published and without a similar condition including this condition being imposed on the subsequent purchaser.

Design by Buzzdesignz

Published by The Roaring Lion Newcastle LTD.

ISBN: 978-1-913636-92-0

Email:
books@theroaringlionnewcastle.com

Website:
www.theroaringlionnewcastle.com

Dedication

This book is dedicated to God Almighty, the giver of life and destiny and also to my parents, Mr. and Mrs. Gabriel Akinyemi, who have filled a great vacuum since I was a little boy.

Table of Contents

ACKNOWLEDGEMENTS

This book would probably only have existed in a dream without the assistance of some highly important individuals that I would like to appreciate here.

To my brother and mentor, Tolu' A. Akinyemi, I owe you a great deal of gratitude for all your input right from A–Z of this book. You took your time to guide me through each stage of writing the book in spite of your busy daily schedule. You are such a wonderful and selfless man, thank you so much.

I equally want to thank the editor, Hungry Bookstore, who took her time to read through the manuscript for necessary corrections and advice. Your labour of love is well appreciated.

I specially thank my wife and daughter, Sarah and Tiwatope, for standing by me through thick and thin in the process of putting my thoughts together. Thank you for always taking care of the home. I love you, my ladies.

My sincere gratitude also goes to my parents, Mr. and Mrs. Gabriel Akinyemi, for all you have been. You sought me out of the dark, brought me into the light, and made the best out of me. You are indeed God sent.

Lastly, I appreciate all my friends and family who supported me in one way or another in the pursuit of this dream. I love you all.

INTRODUCTION

The saddest, and ironically, most beautiful thing about life is that, when we are born, apart from the socialisation we receive that make us members of society, we have no template to map out and live out our life. We live, get good jobs, marry, have children, but we do all this in the face of constant existential crisis. We battle with so many questions throughout our days: What is life? What am I doing here? How can I make the most of my life? and many others...

To answer these questions, we turn to books, religion and philosophy. Some don't even make any attempt to try to figure out life. One thing is certain and unifies us all – we all have questions as to how we can live life meaningfully.

This book is my attempt to answer some of these questions that we all have. No, I do not claim an expertise on the matter of life and living. But as an introspective being, I have my thoughts, backed up with years of finding answers to some of the issues we face in life. And this is why I have written this book, that you, my dear reader, may find answers, or something close, as you turn these pages.

In this book, I lay out principles, some counterintuitive, as to how we can make the best of our lives. It is my joy and desire that, at the end of this book, you find answers, closure, and principles to lay hold of in order to live life to the fullest.

Chapter One

WHY YOU ARE UNHAPPY

True happiness is... to enjoy the present, without anxious dependence upon the future... – Lucius Annaeus Seneca

Happiness is one of the preoccupations of man. We all want to be happy. It is in the pursuit of happiness that we do a lot of things we do – we strive to make money, find a lover, buy things to satisfy an emotional craving for happiness. Our whole human experience revolves around the sustenance of happiness. And this is perfectly okay.

However, there is a worrisome paradox – many of us have sacrificed our happiness in pursuit of happiness. It sounds ironical, but the truth of this claim is out there for all to see. This paradox has been one of my concerns. I ask myself, Why do people remain unhappy despite all they do to make themselves happy? Why is happiness a fleeting feeling or emotion that seems unsustainable? Is this paradox resolvable?

The topic of unhappiness brings a lot to mind. When you ask if someone is unhappy, the responses you expect to get are lack of money, heartbreak, lack of employment, physical or mental illness, and whatnot. But what if one has all these things and they are healthy, yet still unhappy? How do we reconcile that?

There is a misconception we all have, and this misconception, I believe, is why we are unhappy; we have been socialised to believe that happiness is something we derive from externalities like wealth, the acquisition of property, status, pleasure etc. And so, we pursue these things, but we find out that the more we pursue, the more we have, the more we want to have. It's like we are filling a bottomless pit in our soul. As such, we find ourselves in a conundrum of persistent dissatisfaction.

This is not to say that wealth, fame, success, and all those things are bad in and of themselves, or the chasing after them, but it is to dismantle before our eyes the concept that having them automatically equals happiness. In this age, lots of people blindly chase after these things to the exclusion of everything else, burning energy, steam, and making a whole lot of unnecessary, drastic sacrifices along the way, only for them to get to the point they had been hoping for and see that the elusive happiness they seek is still a mere mirage and they find themselves lost.

Talking about happiness, Dane Maxwell in his book, *Start from Zero*, points out the existential question he asked that made him lose an internship position one week before the end of the job: "Are you happy?"

According to him, he was at a dinner organized by the company, and he was sitting with a young employee who had a wedding band on his finger. They got to chatting and the responses Dane got concerning this young man's life, how he only got to spend one week of every month with his wife, made Dane sad and scared. He looked around the table at the seemingly successful people that he was hoping to be like one day and whom he was tailoring his life after, and he didn't see any happiness on their faces. He could not help but subconsciously blurt out, "Is nobody happy at this job?"

At the table were also the seniors, top executives, and a partner who seemed to have it all: awards, luxury houses and rides, vacations in exotic places, and mouth-watering pay. The answers they gave him that day were vague at best, and it got him thinking if it was all worth the stress of going through the dogged process of pursuing success, seeing how bland and unfulfilling their lives were. He got fired the very next day for asking this major, important question, but he would later go on to build several multi-million companies while focusing on personal happiness as a goal in all he did.

What then is this happiness we are talking about? What does it mean to be happy? Or is happiness just an elusive abstraction? If wealth, family, love, marriage, and success equal happiness, why then are those who have all of that unhappy? If a lack of wealth and success is happiness, then why do those who don't have them find themselves sad, bitter, and broken? This question of unhappiness and seeking happiness will constitute a major subplot of this book as we try to understand what it means to live by the script.

Generally, happiness is usually meant to mean a mental or emotional state that embodies pleasant, positive emotions like contentment, intense joy, and peace. Psychology researcher Sonja Lyubomirsky, in her 2007 book, *The How of Happiness*, describes happiness as "the experience of joy, contentment, or positive well-being, combined with a sense that one's life is good, meaningful and worthwhile."

Aristotle, the great Greek Philosopher, envisages happiness as the highest desire and ambition of all human beings, and the way to reach it is through virtue, such as that if one cultivates within oneself the highest virtues, he or she will reach happiness. Another philosopher, Nietzsche, explains happiness as the idea of having vital strength and a fighting spirit, and demonstrating them by overcoming obstacles and creating original ways to live life. And there are many – thousands more – definitions of happiness and what it means to be happy.

But Slavoj Žižek, on happiness as a paradox state, says that being happy is a matter of opinion and not the truth. There is no universal truth or definition of happiness. It is subjective and unique to each person. Even as someone poor thinks wealth would make them happy, a few wealthy people might look at their seemingly loving families and feel that being wealthy has robbed them of that love that they would see as happiness. And so, the circle goes on and on.

Why are you unhappy? There are different reasons why people find themselves in this conundrum that is unhappiness. Psychologists agree that behavioural patterns and patterns in the things we think – cognitive patterns – are the basis of different emotional patterns, including unhappiness, and we will be looking at several that cause unhappiness as I try to make the list as encompassing as possible.

- **Worry**

This constitutes a major reason why many people are unhappy and living a life of sadness and depression. You worry a lot about a lot of things, both in your control and not, and that robs you of your joy. Some people have become so used to worrying that they begin to see negativity and fear in everything around them and in what they do, which can lead to a whole lot more than just taking away their happiness. You worry about what to eat, what to wear, the future, your job, and many other things, so much so that you begin to feel like you are bearing the weight of the world and you become a shadow of yourself.

If we liken the problem to wood that caught fire, then worry is like the oil you pour on that fire again and again, turning it into a raging inferno as you continue to engage it. What worry does is create an inner turmoil that freezes you and makes you unable to act. Your brain dwells so much on the problem, on the things you see not going so well, that you cannot think clearly enough in order to take the necessary decisions to deal with them and make changes so the negative outcome never happens.

When you worry, you tend to dwell in the negative energy of a problem, a behaviour that prevents you from seeing light in anything else, which then makes you sad, melancholic, and withdrawn.

You must understand that you cannot control everything, mistakes are bound to happen, problems are bound to occur, but you can change your perception as to how you see them and engage it. Worrying has never and will never solve any problem, it would only exaggerate it more than it really is.

- **Comparison**

Theodore Roosevelt, a onetime president of the United States of America, says it emphatically like this: "Comparison is the thief of joy." Following the same line of reasoning, Betty Jemmy Chung goes on to say, "Comparison with myself brings improvement, comparison with others brings discontent."

Comparing yourself with others is the greatest disservice you could ever do to yourself. It robs you of your happiness, makes you sad and melancholy, and causes you to lose sight of what is really important in the big picture of things, which also makes you susceptible to mistakes.

Social media and the way people exhibit their life on it has made it appear as if everyone is winning, as if everyone seems happy, posting only those good, well-edited, happy moments. This has a lot of other people feeling like they are missing something important and wanting to measure up. You log into social media and see your friend from secondary school or university seemingly making big waves; you watch people that you used to know to be either on the same level with you, or even below you, doing big things, and then you begin to compare yourself to them, bemoaning your own seemingly lesser achievements.

Always comparing yourself to others will put you in a state of consistent discontent; it will have you running blindly when you should still be building a solid foundation; it will make you take foolish decisions to prove to yourself and others that you too are making it in life and not losing out of whatever they might be having, all of which will harm your future.

Everyone has a different path in life, different opportunities, circumstances and journey. Understand this and have peace and happiness. Rather than comparing yourself with others, always compare yourself with yourself! The best approach when seeing others making big waves is to get inspired and let it propel you to take reasonable steps towards securing the future you want for yourself. Study your weaknesses and try to improve on them, focus on your strength and further capitalize on them, and in all, never take any decisions to prove anything to anyone that wouldn't bring you fulfilment.

- **Lack of gratitude**

This here is another key reason for unhappiness – lack of gratitude!

Most times, people tend to focus on the things they don't have, believing their happiness to be dependent on achieving the next big thing. But the truth is, by the time they get what they want, they again set their sights towards something bigger than that, going through a perpetual continuum of wanting more and more. These are the kind of people that would have the ability to eat three times each day without any stress and still be bothered that they didn't have dessert to go with it, and then that becomes a major source of concern. Or even looking at the bigger picture, they own houses in good environments but are much more concerned about the fact that it isn't big enough, it doesn't have a pool, Jacuzzi and what not.

But there are people out there that do not have a quarter of what some people have!

That is not to say that it is not good to want more – to want to do better than you already have – but not to the extent that it becomes a big weight on your mind that stops you from actually realizing how blessed you are. Having big goals and vision is great, but tying your happiness to future successes that may or may not come will stop you from finding joy in the life you live today.

If you have a roof over your head, a reasonable job or a vocation to lead a nice life with your family, then you are better off than a substantial part of the population.

Amy Collete, in her book, *The Gratitude Connection*, says, "Gratitude is a powerful catalyst for happiness. It's the spark that lights a fire of joy in your soul."

We all need to learn to be grateful for what we have, celebrating the seemingly small wins and understanding that, although we are not where we want to be, we are not where we used to be.

- **Lack of exercise, chronic inactivity, and unhealthy living**

When you exercise, your body releases chemicals called endorphins that react with the receptors in your brain and reduce your perception of pain. What endorphins basically do is spark positive feelings in the body that help you develop a positive outlook on life.

Technology has made it such that an increasing number of job positions are becoming flexible; you can work from home, and you don't need to go through much stress. Many people spend their whole days on the chair, couch, and bed, moving only to carry out essential needs like taking a bath, using the toilet, and getting food to eat.

Just like we have shown that endorphins bring positive energy, researchers have gone further to study and show that physical activity and nutrition are fundamentally linked to happiness. Physical activity is said to bring about a whole new view for a person of his or her personality, boosting their self-confidence and emotional stability, encouraging a positive body image, decreasing anxiety and depression as well as feelings of hostility. In the same vein, diet is said to be linked with improved mood and happiness. This is why we have the popular saying: "You are what you eat."

- **Pursuit of materialism**

While it is important to generate wealth and be rich, it is not all there is to life and living. Perchance you were told that tomorrow was your last day on earth, would you be more concerned about making more money or turn your focus to connecting with some people and having creative experiences?

Lack of wealth serves as a major reason for unhappiness. There are so many things you want for comfort; you thirst to live a comfortable and secure life – to purchase those things you deem important, like a house, a car, and many other needs, but there is no money to fund your wants and so sadness sets in. There is also the erroneous belief that, in the pursuit of wealth, one needs to forgo happiness till a later time when you have achieved all you dream of, which is not so.

As we try to chase our dreams and seek to create wealth, we must learn that it is okay to be happy, even as we struggle towards success. We must not let our circumstances and what we are going through define us, but a positive attitude is necessary to help us forge through the trying times.

- **Hanging around unhappy/negative people**

A popular proverb says, "Birds of a feather flock together." People naturally carry energy around them, energy that can be negative or positive, and these energies have a way of rubbing off on each other. Hanging around unhappy people and complainers is bad news because they wallow in their problems and fail to focus on solutions, and in the process, seek to drag you into their problems.

In the same vein, there are also pessimists who never see anything good in any situation; they only see the bad – the negative sides of life. You must be careful in your dealings with such a group of people because, before you know it, sooner or later, you will begin to think as they do. Their words, most times, act as a self-fulfilling prophecy because expecting things to go wrong only makes it more likely to be so, and if it doesn't go wrong, you will only see how it could have gone wrong and just predicate your success on luck.

You need to be intentional about the people you follow and surround yourself with; fill your circle with people who inspire you, make you want to be better, and to be you. Anyone who makes you feel anxious, fearful, unloved, worthless, or concerned with making you their carbon copy is not worth being around.

- **Playing the blame game/being too fixated on being in control**

This consists of two opposites. It is hard to be happy if you feel you are not in control of your life and that you must behave according to other people's expectations. You may have a pattern you want your life to follow, a way you want to act, but reality proves different in a way where you see yourself conforming to certain things you don't want. Or you feel that nagging desire to control other people's behaviour.

You will find yourself in a perpetual state of unhappiness if you are like this, as there is only little you can control in the big picture, and that is yourself. You cannot determine other people's behaviour or what the world brings to your table.

There is also the act of blaming others and the circumstances in which you find yourself, which doesn't allow one to be able to move forward and make sound decisions going onwards.

Life doesn't always go the way you want it to, and the best way to spend time is to make your time count. Instead of trying to control that which you cannot, control that which you can, which is yourself; discipline yourself, set result-oriented goals, and take the necessary steps towards being the person you want to be.

- **Neglecting to set goals**

Goal-setting is very key to fulfilment. Having goals gives you something to run after, in addition to hope and a vision of a better future. Working towards those goals gives you a sense of purpose that then makes you feel good about yourself and your abilities.

Lack of goals will make you seem like a ship floundering in a large ocean, lost and clueless, with no sense of direction. And you will spend the whole of your life wondering why things never seem to change.

It is sacrosanct to set goals for yourself that are challenging, concise, measurable, and driven by your values. It provides a sense of purpose and achievement as you begin to reach the rungs you have set for yourself.

- **Fear**

There is no doubting the fact that danger exists, but fear is, most times, a lingering emotion that is powered by your imagination. Fear can come in different shapes and sizes; fear of failure, fear of the future, fear of taking risks, fear of death, and the list goes on and on.

Fear stops you from becoming the best you can be, forcing you to retract yourself into a shell of protection that you have built consciously or subconsciously in order to protect you from its realities. What this does is begins to fester and kill you from inside while you are still alive, making you a shadow of who you are supposed to be.

We must learn to live a life without fear and face the world, circumstances, and challenges that face us with a mind of courage and a spirit that overcomes. Then you will see that the victories that come from challenging and facing these obstacles will be the most gratifying ever.

- **You are stuck in the past and scared of the future**

Just like fear, this is just the product of your mind. There is nothing you can do to change your past – not feeling guilty about it, dwelling on it, thinking of what you could have changed; and no amount of anxiety can change the future.

To be happy, you must learn to make the best of the moment, accept your past and make peace with it. You must also accept the uncertainty of the future and not place unnecessary expectations on yourself.

- **Seeking validation**

If you are the kind of person who always seeks validation from other people, then it is certain that you will always live an unhappy life. Human wants are insatiable; you can never fully satisfy any one person no matter how hard you try. You must learn to live your life with you in focus – your fulfilment, your growth, your peace of mind – even at the pain of being ostracized from some circles, which will not be easy. But if you are happy with what you do and where you now find yourself, you will find that the pain of being pushed away because you put yourself first will not be as much as that you would experience just following the flow.

- **Lack of sleep and relaxation**

Lack of sleep naturally makes one grumpy and cold; it affects your overall mood, likewise with a lack of relaxation. Science proffers that eight hours of sleep is needed every twenty-four hours, and this is very important to note. Try to take time out of that tight schedule of yours to sleep, go to the park or relaxation centres, to picnics with family and loved ones, and you will see yourself refreshed and brimming with positive energy.

- **You don't like your job**

Lack of job satisfaction can rob you of happiness, especially when you feel no connection with what you do, or you feel underpaid, or the work is monotonous, or the boss is harsh and unfeeling, and myriad other reasons.

The best way to remedy this is to begin working towards your passion and not just a paycheck. Doing what you love has a way of motivating you to be able to overcome obstacles and challenges, making happiness spring forth in your heart as you are doing what makes you tick.

***

Most of what people do today, most of our struggles and running around, is centred around our search for happiness, and so we build constructs around what happiness should be, what culture and society have determined it to be, and we still do not get it.

Happiness is an intentional decision – a choice. It takes a renewal of the mind and a reorientation of your thought processes to bring it to birth. Like we explained in the preceding paragraphs, we need to understand those patterns that make us unhappy and reconfigure our perceptions towards them. No matter the situation, you can always choose to be happy. No one can take that from you if you so determine.

Chapter Two

THE 'MORE' TRAP

*As long as you think more is better, you will
never be satisfied. – Richard Carlson*

In our search for fulfilment, we have come to
believe certain narratives or myths on what it
means to be truly fulfilled. These narratives have
become widely acceptable and ingrained in us. We
believe that adding more to what we already have
or don't have would make our life better and, in
effect, make us fulfilled and happier. And this
belief – that we need to have more – pushes us to
the point of discontent and dissatisfaction; it
blinds us from appreciating what we already have
and being content with our life. The result is that
we don't see that we are drawing away from the
happiness that was the basis of these pursuits in
the first place.

The 'more' trap takes its premise from our
environment, which influences our behaviour and

desires, the culture of the society we find ourselves, the knowledge we have acquired over time, and our basic instincts as humans as it relates to our 'needs' and 'wants'. To understand the foundation and driving force of the 'more' trap, we must first understand the link between our 'wants' and our 'needs', and how society and our minds have developed the 'more' narrative.

'Want' is what we wish for to make our lives better, pleasurable, and comfortable, while 'need', on the other hand, is a necessity on which human beings are dependent for existence – oxygen, food, safety, etc.

'Wants' and 'needs' constitute the basis of our desires and behaviour, and they, directly and indirectly, shape us as humans. Hokky Situngkir says, "Our desire for things can come from what we want and what we need… the need and the want are both shaping the way we keep on living in a most pleasant way." He was relating happiness to "the balance between what and how we desire things as we want and need them."

The growth, development, and changes in our environment also play an important role in shaping our wants and needs, and subsequently, our desires and behaviour. In the pre-modern or Stone Age, for example, human needs and wants revolved around safety, security, shelter, and food. Although our needs in this age are not so different from what they were in that age, globalization and technology have broadened the scope of what we think should constitute our needs, and what makes for a happy and fulfilled life is being redefined daily. This makes people chase blindly after the dream life. The 'American Dream' is an example of a standard of happiness and what makes for a fulfilled life.

Behavioural scientists posit happiness to be a 'want' and not amongst the basic 'needs', but happiness is at the root of other 'wants' that drive human pursuit.

The 'more' trap is a narrative that pushes us to see the satisfaction of our numerous insatiable wants as a basis for happiness, thereby propelling us towards filling that gaping hole that is our desires in a bid to achieve fulfilment.

This trap is the root of dissatisfaction. It has many people chasing blindly after material pursuits without rest.

For example, shelter is a basic human need. You worked hard and were able to buy yourself a house for your family in a nice and serene environment. You realise that the satisfaction you got from purchasing your dream house does not last; it's not long before you begin to scheme for ways to get a bigger house so that the children can each get a room and bigger space to play around, a swimming pool and space for a garden.

There would never be an end to what you want, especially as new changes occur every minute, and what you wanted and got is improved upon or newer versions developed, making it so you find yourself in a never-ending loop of wanting more.

In the words of Tana French, "Our entire society is based on discontent. People wanting more and more, being constantly dissatisfied with their homes, their bodies, their décor, their clothes, everything – taking it for granted that that's the whole point of life."

In a cross-section of a society consisting of different classes – apart from the very wealthy who can easily float above basic economic constraints without being outrightly affected by its unpredictability and trends – those in the upper class down to those in the lowest of classes can always be found similarly complaining of the increasingly high standard of living and how they are always left with close to nothing before the next paycheck arrives, irrespective of the amount of money they make.

What this does is have people chasing doggedly after promotions and the increased paycheck that comes with it, or chasing after expanding their business and raking in more profit so that they can satisfy their wants. But as more money comes in, so does the want increase.

The 'more' trap is a lie – a capitalist construct designed to keep people perpetually focused on consumption as the means to achieve true happiness and fulfilment.

These myths are further propagated by brands and companies who promote their products by exploiting our desires and appealing to our sensibilities with content that sells the idea that more is better, showing visuals and telling you how their products can help you attain the happiness you seek and what happiness should look like. Philip Slater, author of *The Pursuit of Loneliness*, saw through this when he said, "Our economy is based on spending billions to persuade people that happiness is buying things, and then insisting that the only way to have a viable economy is to make things for people to buy so they will have jobs and get enough money to buy things."

There is also the role of the mind and how it enables the 'more' trap myth. Our mind, which embodies our thoughts, has a way of thinking up and ascribing value to material things beyond necessity; things that we want to get or achieve become a preoccupation in our mind over time, slowly starting to look like a giant obstacle that must be overcome, making us strive, run and toil to do so. On getting these things, however, we see that we don't experience the satisfaction we thought we would have. Or if we do, it lasts for just a while.

Master Ramana Maharshi, a renowned Brahman teacher, says, "The mind is such that it shows a tiny mustard seed to be a huge mountain until it is attained. As soon as it has been attained, the mountain appears as insignificant as a mustard seed."

This is what happens to most of us. Sometimes we feel like 'If I don't get this new phone, new clothes, or this new model of car, then life is not going to be as interesting as it should be'. But after getting them, you see how mundane those things are, that they don't really give you the satisfaction you want. However, our mind has been conditioned in such a way that it won't stay long with this revelation. Immediately, we become dissatisfied with what we have, and we look forward to getting the next big thing. Jaak

Panksepp calls this "the seeking instincts of man." In his book, *Affective Neuroscience*, he argues that, of seven core instincts in the human brain (anger, fear, panic-grief, maternal care, pleasure/lust, play, and seeking), seeking is the most important. The human desire to seek can help make sense of studies that show that achieving major goals or even winning the lottery doesn't cause long-term changes in happiness because, in the process of seeking, exaggerations have so occurred in your mind, so getting the result would not satisfy the craving you have built around the goal.

Various scholars have expounded on the matter that this seeking instinct is a very important and fulfilling activity as it makes life interesting, but we need to understand that the result of seeking is not happiness. It is the nature of the mind to want more, to be dissatisfied and not content.

The 'more' trap has had people finding themselves lost, sad, and depressed at different stages of life, no matter what achievement they have accomplished, and we will take a look at some of the myths of the 'more' trap that we have come to believe and accept, myths that are robbing us of happiness and fulfilment; there are a lot of them.

- **The myth of perfection**

The myth of perfection affects us at various junctures – sometimes creeping into our lives and thought processes subconsciously – and it is one of the most popular myths that the 'more' trap hinges upon, acting as the biggest thief of our happiness and fulfilment.

Psychology Today defines perfectionism as "a personality trait characterized by high expectations and standards." David Heitz goes on further to say that perfectionism and chasing after perfection is usually a learned behaviour, and people with perfectionist tendencies believe that they're only valuable because of what they achieve or what they do for other people, making them always focused on doing more and more, and also expecting the same of other people they enter into any form of relationship and interaction with.

All our life we have been configured and led towards thinking along the lines of perfection in all the things that we do, and to see the rewards attached to the results of our endeavours as synonymous with the emotion of happiness. Growing up, we see our parents trying to raise us as the perfect child; in school, our teachers push us to get perfect grades and behave in a manner they believe is proper; in society, we are led in a way to get along with and relate to others, and there are reward systems and preferential treatment in place for people who conform and come out on top of these expectations. The narrative we have grown up hearing is that you can and should do 'more', you should always strive towards perfection, and only then will you achieve good results that will truly be worthwhile.

Over time, this sense of perfection slowly becomes ingrained in our internal system and mental process such that achieving anything below the bars set by society becomes a cause for alarm, especially in this global age of increased technological advancements where information and culture intertwine with each other. It is in this desire to be perfect that we begin to lose sight of what we truly want and of our personality, and find ourselves conforming to society's definition of happiness and others' expectations of us, thereby short-changing ourselves.

The American businessman Chamath Palihapitiya says, "We curate our lives around this perceived sense of perfection because we get rewarded in these short-term signals: Hearts, likes, thumbs-up. We conflate that with value, and we conflate it with truth, and instead, what it really is – is fake, brittle popularity that is short term and leaves you even more vacant and empty before you did it." Since our behaviours have been tagged with reward and a feeling of specialness over time and we find again and again that our achievements bring us the attention we long for, we strive harder to always feel special and receive that distinction that we hope will make us feel at ease and happy. This pursuit can throw us off from really understanding and embodying our own passions, unique attributes, and overall sense of self.

We all have the perfect picture of what we want our lives to be, what we want our marriages to be – a perfect picture of the goals we pursue and the vision of what we aim to achieve, and this affects our thoughts, actions, and expectations. Growing up, some of us developed ideas of what an ideal spouse should be, especially with the narratives of a perfect gentleman and a beautiful princess being spread about, but imagine when your spouse doesn't have all those things you hoped for even if you truly love them? Or the new seemingly picture-perfect car you just bought is lacking a specification another car has, and then it all begins to look imperfect to you, bringing up reasons for concern.

But is there anything like perfection?

Salvador Dali says, "Have no fear of perfection – you will never reach it." In the same vein, many other great men that we all aspire to be like, such as Winston Churchill, the great inventor Albert Einstein, the brain surgeon Ben Carson, and a whole number of others, have explained how perfection is impossible, and that they have been able to use the idea of how impossible perfection is, in their relationships with others and in understanding themselves, and make the goals they set as realistic as possible.

That is not to say that we should not set standards for ourselves or live a life of principle, but that we should always set attainable goals and not be overwhelmed with the idea of perfection as it robs us of the joys of every little win. There is no universal definition of perfection; what might seem perfect to you might seem not so perfect to another. It is in this same sense that an artist describes everything, even what might seem like a mistake, in a painting or drawing as a 'work of art'.

- **The myth that bigger is better**

In the words of Pearl S. Buck: "Many people lose the small joys in the hope for the big happiness."

The myth that 'bigger is better' is another narrative we have come to accept, in that, whatever we want to do in life, it is better to do it in a very big way – to do it with a bang! Because of this reasoning, many people have built an unhealthy appetite for material possessions and the goals that they want to achieve. Why go for a small car that is affordable and cost-effective when you can get the latest, classiest car with some more months of effort, or through a loan that you would pay overtime?

We have also come to consider spending more money to satiate our wants and needs and following societal trends a means to happiness. This is why we see ourselves chasing after designer clothing, shoes, and accessories, a chase that drains our purse and, in truth, provides very little satisfaction but for the accolades and vain recognition they would bring. Inability to get those bigger, shinier things would constitute a reason for concern and has many either moping around or striving blindly in pursuit of acquiring them.

Society has been so configured in this way that people who even try to live their lives outside this narrative are mocked and ridiculed for being non-conformist and for not being modern, and it takes a personal effort to rise above this belief.

Studies have shown that, in relationships, what counts are not the expensive cars, massive mansions, and even shiny diamonds you get for your spouse, but those little things: the short walks together, the breakfasts in bed, the random texts and messages, those small thoughtful gifts, like a hairpin or set of cufflinks that matches their eye colour... Although big things are also an integral part of what makes love interesting, the smaller, thoughtful things are what really strengthens closeness, loyalty, and strong feelings in a love relationship.

- **The myth that happiness should be postponed to the end**

This is the belief that happiness is the end of all our struggles in life, and that, to be happy, one has to first go through a lot of hard and difficult times, crossing mountains, oceans, and insurmountable obstacles to reach that state. Many have, due to this reason, seen themselves as undeserving of happiness till they hit their set goals, turning themselves into a mindless machine as they strive to do more and more to quickly reach that end and retire into happiness.

In a way, religion has also cemented this claim of happiness coming at the end of your pursuits with the message that this world is not our final destination, but that there is a bigger, better world waiting for us after death, and so many postpone their happiness and spend their life running towards the finish line even as they strive to gain wealth.

The mind works in such a way that if you continue to postpone your feelings of happiness, over time, your mind dulls to the emotion so that even when you attain that goal you seek, you find no sense of happiness and fulfilment in it. In the words of Deepak Chopra: "Life gives you plenty of time to do whatever you want to do if you stay in the present moment." There is enough time to be happy in the present even as you chase your goals and to be happy when you also hit those goals.

- **The myth that you'll be happy as soon as you...**

Often, we often think that we'll be happy as soon as we get married, get a job, get that promotion, move to a new apartment, and so on. But arriving at your destination, because you have already been expecting to reach it, you find that it has already become a part of your happiness and the joy in it becomes rather short-lived.

According to Gretchen Rubin, a writer: "When I find myself focusing overmuch on the anticipated future happiness of arriving at a certain goal, I often remind myself to 'enjoy now'. The fun part doesn't come later, *now* is the fun part." This does not mean that aiming to arrive at that destination or to attain that goal won't bring about happiness, but we must understand that the goal is as important as the process leading to the goal and that one must strive for happiness through it all.

***

When I talk about the 'more' trap, I am not saying that we shouldn't strive to make the most of our life and live to the fullness of our potential, no; I am not saying that we should be content with mediocrity when we can do more and be more; we should strive because we cannot live a fulfilled, satisfied life if we subject ourselves to an average life when we could have been more.

The message I am trying to pass on is – we should know when our pursuit of our wants is robbing us of inner satisfaction, when it is blinding us from seeing what truly matters. We must learn how to balance want and happiness, know when to be content and when to look for more. And more importantly, we should know that while ambition is noble, while we strive to create a life of comfort for ourselves, all these things in and of themselves might not bring us to a state of lasting fulfilment and satisfaction.

The 'more' trap is like cancer cells that spread, casting a shadow of discontent on every iota of happiness in a person's life.

The key to overcoming the 'more' trap is contentment – to be satisfied with what you have and try to find happiness in those seemingly little things. We must develop and discipline our minds to see that if our 'needs' are already met, then the pursuit of 'wants' shouldn't sap our life of the happiness, satisfaction, and fulfilment that we deserve.

Chapter Three

THE THINGS THAT MATTER

The things that matter most must never be at the mercy of the things that matter least. – Johann Wolfgang von Goethe

The fuel that drives success in life is ambition, dedication, being focused on one's goals, and zeroing in on their pursuit. This is the secret behind the success of high achievers – they are people who have made countless sacrifices on the altar of success.

However, the bane of ambition is that, most times, we lack a sense of balance. We become so totally driven in the pursuit of success that we overinvest in one aspect of our life and under-invest in another, as if one is more important than the other, as if one matters more than the other. We quickly forget that life is more than our career and that success in our career, as much as it could bring one happiness, does not override the need to invest in our relationships.

And this inability to manage our investment (our time, energy, and dedication), this inability or unwillingness to rightly appropriate our investment, in all aspects of our life is what brings about regrets later in life.

It is easy to fall into this trap of investing more in our career than in our relationships. This is because whatever investment we make into our career always yields immediate results – we get that promotion we want, that pay rise, and our name is on the lips of everyone that matters in our line of work. As such, we tend to prioritise our career over our relationships because the investment in relationships does not always yield immediate results. And it is easy not to be mindful of this lack of appropriate investment in our relationship when one is providing materially in the relationship. The material provision becomes all that seems to matter, but it is not.

For many of us, we do not see the need to invest in our relationship as much as we do in our career until it is too late. By the time we realise that, despite our achievement and success, we will be alone. The children you did not give your time to will have become adults; you will be retired and then yearn for a relationship with them, but they can't give you one even if they want to because there is no foundation for it. One realises too late in life that success in one's career cannot take the place of having fulfilling and meaningful relationships, and that what will give us deeper, long-lasting joy is the intimate relationships we have cultivated over time.

The truth is, we live in a world where emphasis is placed more on success in career and wealth creation. And it has made it easier for people to sacrifice their relationships in pursuit of this.

It is not that it is wrong to be ambitious or to want to be at the top career-wise; it is that there are things that must not be sacrificed for that end – your relationship is one.

What fuels this attitude of sacrificing relationship for a career is that we think that the more we focus on our career at the expense of other aspects of our lives, the more fulfilled we will be. This is a misconception. Rob Cross, co-founder and research director of the Connected Commons, discovered that happiness and fulfilment in a career depend on how well one invests in his or her relationships.

The reason for this is not farfetched; man is a social animal, and his emotional health, which in turn influences other aspects of his life, depends on the quality of his social connections. That is, social connection plays a vital role in fostering one's sense of purpose and wellbeing.

This, therefore, shows that sacrificing social connections and relationship for the sake of fulfilment at work or career or business is a disservice to oneself.

> *The happiest moments of my life have been the few which I have passed at home in the bosom of my family. – Thomas Jefferson*

One of the most disheartening stories I have heard in my life is the story of Joyce Vincent, the woman who died alone in her room and no one knew until two years later when her bank account from which her bills were automatically debited ran dry. Two years and no one came to visit this woman.

The reality is that a lot of us are like Joyce Vincent; we are not dead, but we are walking corpses, dying inside out from loneliness and depression, being crushed from the weight of the burdens we bear alone – all because we do not have deeper, more meaningful relationships in our life, or because we hide from those who love us; or worse still, they are too busy with their lives to notice us.

This is not the way man is designed to live. We are innately wired for communal living; we strive and flourish by having deeper and meaningful relationships. It is the joy and happiness that we derive from these relationships that give us a sense of purpose, a reason to want to pursue and attain a goal. Because, when all is said and done, what really matters is our relationships – how meaningful they are.

I am not saying that our career is not important or that we should neglect it, no. Rather, what I am driving at is the need for us to learn how to prioritise what matters and place importance on it. It is the need for us to place value on our relationships, to take the time to build and maintain meaningful relationships because, when the storms of life hit as they are wont to, what we will fall back on is not our job, business, or career, it is the people around us, our relationships.

> *The memories we make with our family is everything. – Candace Cameron Bure*

So, having established the fact that our life is beyond our career, that the quality of our relationships determines how happy and fulfilled we are in our career, it is, therefore, necessary to know how to build and maintain these deep, meaningful, intimate relationships.

Like I said earlier, we get tempted to direct our investments into other things at the expense of our relationships because the rewards those other things give us is immediate; this is also true of the consequences of not investing in our relationships – they are not immediate. Also, because our work is naturally designed to be demanding of our time while our friends and family might not want to demand for our time, we often fail to appropriate investment into these relationships. Clayton Christensen puts it this way in *How Will You Measure Your Life*:

> *I genuinely believe that relationships with family and close friends are one of the greatest sources of happiness in life. It sounds simple, but like any important investment, these relationships need consistent attention and care. But there are two forces that will be constantly working against this happening. First, you'll be routinely tempted to invest your resources elsewhere – in things that will provide you with a more immediate payoff. And second, your family and friends rarely shout the*

loudest to demand your attention. They love you and they want to support your career, too. That can add up to neglecting the people you care about most in the world. The theory of good money, bad money explains that the clock of building a fulfilling relationship is ticking from the start. If you don't nurture and develop those relationships, they won't be there to support you if you find yourself traversing some of the more challenging stretches of life, or as one of the most important sources of happiness in your life.

This is why we cannot leave the building and maintaining of intimate, meaningful relationships to chance; we must, instead, be deliberate about it. We must prioritise our relationships and put in the effort to building and maintaining them. This requires us to learn to invest our resources into our relationship, and this includes our time.

The best thing we can give people is our time. And all too often, time is a resource that we are not always ready to give. In this fast-paced, highly demanding world, it is not uncommon to see husbands and wives who have no time for their children, not to mention their friends. These are parents who would leave for work early in the morning and come home late in the night. By the time they are back from work, the kids are in bed already. They do not have time to talk with their spouse either. And so, while they seem to have a flourishing career, the home is an empty shell, void of love and warmth.

The reasons for the dysfunction in society can be traced to this – people coming from loveless homes where relationships are not valued. And so, these people go into the world and begin to form toxic relationships, and the cycle of toxicity in relationships continues.

One of the ways to figure out what you prioritise and value is how much time you give to it. Some people would say they love their family and friends, but they do not give them their time. How then do they prove this love? We are not who we say we are; we are what we do. If you love and value your family, your relationships, you will invest your time in them.

True, we need to get work done so that we can provide for our family, and this can be very demanding of our time, so this is where we learn to appropriate our time wisely on the things that matter. For Clayton Christensen, it is rushing home immediately after work to meet his children. For others, it is spending the weekend with their family. You have to create a system that works for you; if you don't, you will give no time to the people that matter, and then create a distance that cannot be closed.

You have to give time to what you prioritise. This may require that you deny yourself some things so you can spend time with your family, but in the end, the sacrifice will be worth it.

Closely related to time is attention. Let me paint the picture of a modern family to you: in a cream-coloured sitting room, the TV is on. You can see the father and mother seated beside each other, the kids too; one is on the Persian rug in the middle of the sitting room, the other is coiled on one of the couches. But instead of talking with each other, the father has his laptop on his lap, engrossed in work he brought home from the office. The mother is busy attending to customers online. The child on the couch is on her phone, chatting with her friends on social media while the other kid is watching the program on the TV. Yes, I know people can get tired of talking and can be at home, at peace in the silence of each other's presence, but go to the same family again and again, and this is the picture you see all the time. They are together in the flesh, but their minds, their attention is far apart. There is an invisible wall between them, you see; this wall is their mobile devices. And no, the villain is not these devices or social media as we are wont to shift the blame to anything but ourselves; the guilty are each member of the family, the father and mother taking a larger chunk of the blame.

The time invested in your relationship is of no use if you do not corroborate it with attention. It is not just spending time with them – the memories we create are determined by what we spend the time doing. Are we on our devices every time we are together, or do we have meaningful conversations, play, and have fun?

Paying attention is important in maintaining intimate relationships. Taking note of the things that are important to our family and friends is one way of paying attention; it could be seemingly little things like complimenting them when they get a new haircut, knowing when they have changed their perfume or lipstick. And listening, especially listening. There is no greater form of attention than when we listen. It is not only a sign of respect – another resource we must invest in our relationships – it is proof that we are paying attention as well.

Another resource we must invest in our relationship is our commitment. No relationship can survive a lack of commitment. Unfortunately, commitment is a resource a lot of people find hard to invest in their relationship. They lack a sense of commitment, and the reason for this is that they do not want to be responsible. But a relationship cannot survive when one party is not committed, when one party is always the one receiving and does not offer anything in return. Apart from sheer irresponsibility, the reason for this lack of commitment is the misconception that we need to find someone who will make us happy. While this is true, it often tilts the responsibility to the other person. No, being in a relationship is not just about being with someone who will make us happy; it is more about finding someone who we can make happy and being committed to making them happy. If we all approach relationships from this perspective, if we all strive to make the other person happy, instead of just being the one in search of happiness, then we will have more stable, healthier relationships, which will improve our overall wellness and satisfaction in other aspects of our lives.

We do not only invest commitment; we must make sacrifices too. Because what actually strengthens our commitment in our relationship is the sacrifices we make because of it. While money is essential to raise a family and maintain relationships, it cannot strengthen relationships as much as commitment and sacrifice can. This is why you see a family of middle and low income who are very happy, whose home is filled with warmth and love, while there are rich homes where daggers are always flying. The reason for this is that there is commitment and sacrifice fuelled by love in one and absent in another.

The best things we can give our children, spouses, and friends is not money, though that is important; not gifts, although that too is needed; the best thing we can gift our family are those abstract things like our time, commitment, and sacrifice. These are the things by which love is measured. Love is duty. It runs deeper than feelings and emotions; love is a duty, and commitment to this duty of love is what helps us derive happiness from our relationships, and this, in turn, gives us purpose and fulfilment that permeates other aspects of our lives.

***

The things that matter in life is our relationships. The happiness we derive from our work, career, or anything else is transient. We can be replaced elsewhere in life, but to our family and friends, we are hardly replaceable.

We must appropriate our resources to things that matter. Our sacrifices, time, and commitment should be invested in that which is worthy of them. When the trying and dark times of life befall us, it is relationships, family and friends, that we fall back to. And no celebration is complete without family and friends to share it with.

Chapter Four

LIVING BY THE SCRIPT

*Anything and everything you have experienced
has been purposeful; it has brought you to where
you are now. – Iyanla Vanzant*

There is an existential question that persists, that men keep asking, and that is: Who am I? And why am I here? What is my purpose here on Earth? Beneath these questions is a search for meaning, a reason for existence. This is because, without a reason and purpose for existence, without an intrinsic knowledge of who one is and why he or she is here on Earth, life is haphazard and living becomes meaningless.

I believe that the purpose of life is a life of purpose, that a man is yet to live until he finds something to live for. Almost everyone believes this to be true, yet they live their life without a thorough grasp of what purpose is; they are successful but not fulfilled, rich but without a sense of meaning. And as such, they yearn for something more, something to satiate this thirst for meaning, for purpose, a reason for their existence on Earth. And this quest for purpose shows that, in the core of the human soul, man wants to live for something; he seeks meaning, and he wants to do something that makes a lasting impact on the world.

This intention is noble. But when we talk about purpose, it is often said to be that one thing that one was created to do – that one thing that one must discover. And so, the question that needs to be asked is: Does a particular job, career, or talent define what one's purpose is? Are we here on Earth for just a specific thing? Is purpose predetermined such that we just have to discover it?

It is important to answer this question because purpose is often said to be tied to one's passion, talent, and gifts. If that is true, what becomes of multitalented people? What becomes of people with one or more passion and gifts? How do they know which particular talent, gift, or passion is where their purpose lies?

The question needs to be answered not just because of people with many talents, passion, and gifts, but for those who have no idea what we want to be or do with our lives, people who are not certain that their life has meaning and purpose because they feel what they are doing is not gigantic in the grand scheme of things, that they are not making impact; they are afraid they are not living by purpose and are frustrated as a result of this.

***

The truth is that everything we know about purpose has stemmed from certain misconceptions. And one will keep asking the same questions – *What is my purpose? And how do I find it?* – if these misconceptions are not cleared up.

The first misconception is that we need to find our purpose.

When people ask, *How do I find purpose?*, what they mean most of the time is – What is that big thing I can do that will make an impact on the world, that will make me popular?

While these intentions are good, they are not really about purpose. First of all, we do not find purpose; instead, our purpose is something we create. If this is true, it means that we can create purpose from whatever it is that we are doing. This calls for a mindset shift.

Another thing about purpose is that it does not need to be something spectacular. A lot of people are waiting to do something big and exciting; they are waiting to touch a million lives before they can say they have found and fulfilled their purpose. This is wrong because not all of us will do something big. What matters is the ability to do the seemingly little things with a touch of excellence and selflessness, and the ability to create purpose out of that.

When I talk about creating purpose from the little things we do, I like to share this inspiring story of the US president John F. Kennedy and a janitor at NASA's headquarters.

In 1961, President John F. Kennedy visited NASA's headquarters. There, he met a janitor who was mopping the floor. He introduced himself to the janitor and proceeded to ask the janitor what he did at NASA. The janitor replied, "I am helping to put a man on the moon."

This janitor's answer shows an impressive mindset that we all must have – his ability to tie the seeming little thing he was doing with the grand purpose of NASA – his ability to create meaning and purpose from it. We need to learn this. A lot of people would have answered President Kennedy: "I am a janitor here; I mop, sweep and clean." They would not be wrong, but that answer shows that they are disconnected from the grand purpose of where they are working and that they do not see a greater purpose to what they are doing, and therefore, not deriving meaning from it.

When it comes to finding meaning in what we do, our aim must shift from deriving meaning from what we do to making what we do meaningful. Making what we do meaningful is essential and it determines whether we will find fulfilment in it or not.

Purpose is often said to be that one thing one was created to do. Well, it is not. Against the idea of a specific, predetermined purpose, purpose cannot be articulated into one single, specific thing. This idea of a single purpose has confused a lot of multi-talented people who have questioned: *Which of my talents is my purpose tied to?*

Many times, people become stranded at the junction of decision because they cannot settle for one. Some end up pursuing that one thing they are convinced is their purpose at the expense of other things they could have been good at.

Also, our sense of purpose changes as we grow and go through changes of our own in life. Yes, there is no specific, predetermined purpose; our purpose is not static, instead, our sense of purpose goes through changes throughout our lifetime. What this means is that you are not just created to be one thing or to do one thing, that your purpose and existence, the sense of meaning and fulfilment, is not tied to one particular thing. An understanding of this will make one embrace wholesome living, a life that is not limited to just one thing.

We cannot talk about purpose without talking about identity. Because one develops a sense of purpose as they become attuned with their identity. And just like purpose, the unravelling of one's identity is not a one-time event; it is a continuous thing. We are ever-evolving beings; we are continually changed and influenced by what we expose ourselves to, our experiences, our education, our environment. And this constant evolution is a sign of true living. If you are not changing and evolving, you are not living. As one's understanding of identity changes, so does one's sense of purpose.

An example is in order. Remember that time when you were a child and you were asked what you wanted to be in the future? You might have wanted to be a doctor or lawyer, and though you were a child, this choice of career and purpose was influenced by what you were exposed to. However, you got to secondary school, and you discovered new things about yourself. You discovered that you were good at playing instruments, or that you had a passion for filmmaking. And this new discovery changed the course and direction of your life; you stopped wanting to be a lawyer and decided to learn filmmaking because that was what gave your life meaning, that was where you thought you could create something that would impact the world. Your purpose changed because of a discovery you made about yourself.

If our purpose is not definite and static, this then means that it is not a destination either. You can create and fulfil purpose at whatever age or point you are. In essence, purpose is something we can revisit and redefine at any point in our lives.

While purpose is a way to derive self-fulfilment, it is more about what one is able to do for others. Purpose is tied to service and not self-glorification. Therefore, when you find a place where you can be of service to people, where you can add value to people, then you can create purpose there.

> *Find what you love and let it kill you. – Charles Bukowski*

Creating purpose and meaning from something is not something we can achieve in a day; it is a continuous process that sometimes requires testing and trials. What we have to do is find something we love to do and create meaning from it. The story of the writer and poet Charles Bukowski comes to mind. After thirty years of writing without getting published – note that he had kept writing all these years while he did other things – he eventually got a publishing deal. When accepting the publishing deal, he said, "I have one of two choices – stay in the post office and go crazy... or stay out here and play at writer and starve. I have decided to starve."

See, he found something he loves – which is not the same as loving what he does all the time – and decided to pursue it.

This brings us to the place of knowing what you want from life and enjoying the risks. A lot of us have an idea of what we love to do, where we can create meaning and find the fulfilment we seek, but we are not ready to embrace the risks and sacrifices it demands. This is why you see people who would have loved to be photographers staying stuck in their jobs at the bank and being unhappy about it. They could not create happiness from what they do, yet they cannot bear the risk of leaving to explore the other thing.

There is a question we might need to ask ourselves in the quest for creating purpose and finding meaning, and the question, like Mark Manson puts it, is: *What kind of pain do I want to have in my life?*

We always relate purpose with happiness and a constant state of nirvana such that we cannot even imagine that something that gives us purpose and meaning could be painful too. But this is not so. While there is an attendant meaning and happiness that comes from finding something to live for, there are also risks and sacrifices we have to make. For the banker wanting to switch to photography, this may mean forgoing the comfort that earning a fat salary at the bank brings. This is why I say finding something you love is not always loving what you do. But you have to ask yourself and decide the kind of pain you are willing to live with for that thing you cannot trade all the riches in this world for, no matter the sacrifice it demands from you.

Like I mentioned earlier, creating purpose also stems from a place of serving others. Yes, it is okay to want to derive happiness from what you do, but one way to create purpose is to find something to do for others instead of yourself. We are not special on Earth – well, except to our family and friends – but we can do something that is significant for other people. Think of yourself as a superhero and ask yourself, *How would I love to save the world?* You can create purpose from solving that problem you see in your street or church, from correcting that dysfunction you see in your school.

What I am trying to say is that creating purpose is not all about oneself; there is a way to find meaning and fulfilment in just helping other people. Creating purpose can stem from finding that thing that is greater than you, that is beyond just yourself.

We cringe at the words 'service' and 'sacrifice' because we are too obsessed with happiness. But if there is one thing I would love to leave you with in this book, it is that life is not about happiness. Happiness is temporary and transient, and as such, it is such a banal thing to base our decisions on. This does not mean that we should leave a sadistic, melancholic life, but that we should seek beyond our happiness; this makes it easier to serve others, which could then, in turn, give us meaning and purpose in life.

I would like to end this chapter with this thought: *It is okay to be clueless.*

I understand the need to find purpose and meaning, but the truth is that, for the most part, we do not know what we want. Instead of giving in to depression and unhappiness because you have yet to find those things you love and create purpose and meaning from them, focus on living instead. Life is not all about happiness, but we cannot live most of our lives being sad and anxious over a lack of purpose and meaning. Once again, the reason for this is that we have been taught that we are special, but can we relax at the thought that we are not and enjoying living instead?

Yes, some people are so sure about what they want to do from the start and are happy and fulfilled for it, but if that is not you, that is perfectly okay.

Yes, a lot of us end up doing just one thing throughout our life, but that is because we only focus on that one thing that brings us fame or makes us rich. People have multiple things that bring them meaning – their family, spouse and children, their pets – outside of that major thing that they are known for.

Moreover, the truth is, a lot of us stumble upon the things that give us meaning just by chance or mistake. It is not that we are dead sure about it from the start. And because our purpose evolves, just like our understanding of who we are and what we want, there are many things in our life that we can create purpose from.

Chapter Five

THE SPRING WITHIN

If you are working on something that you really care about, you don't have to be pushed. The vision pulls you. – Steve Jobs

Most of our actions are driven by a course or goal. We rarely do things without external or internal motivation – something to drive us. There is that thing that makes us tick.

For example, the job you are doing, what drives you may be the need for survival, or the need to make an impact in life. Whatever it is – are you sure that source of motivation will keep you going when push comes to shove?

Perhaps you don't like the word 'motivation' and you attack everything that sounds like 'aspire to perspire', and you argue that nothing motivates you, that you are your own man. You are the captain of your ship, eulogizing yourself with your philosophy. Well, that's cool. But it doesn't mean nothing drives you. Something beloved drives you. For some of us, our experiences so far have been the major wheel that drives us. The truth is, diverse situations we have been in have shaped our perspective about life, inspired certain decisions, and have led to the path some of us walk now.

It is said that: "Every morning in Africa, when a zebra wakes up, it knows it must outrun the fastest lion or it will be killed. Every morning in Africa, when a lion wakes up, it knows it must run faster than the slowest zebra, or it will starve. It doesn't matter whether you're the lion or a zebra – when the sun comes up, you'd better be running." As much as this sounds like an ideal drive for animals, it is wired in humans as a survival instinct. The thing about being motivated by survival alone, living to survive, is that we will never attain a state of self-fulfilment. So, one could live for more than a century and not truly live.

In a world with a population of over 7.6 billion people, billions of people are driven by different things, and their pursuit in life is interwoven with their motivation. Think of motivation as a serum that is injected into a snail to make it faster. Here, one shot of Elon Musk's neural link serum has been injected into a snail, and it can now move as fast as the almighty cheetah. Perhaps that's not imagery; remember when you were promised a reward if you could make a particular grade? Exactly! It drove you to study hard. But did you make it?

Well, I could bet that most people didn't. And this is because extrinsic motivations, like fireworks, eventually die off. After a while, such folks tend to feel unfulfilled and have a high chance of slipping into depression.

Out of the plethora of motivations that can drive a person, the following is a list of elements that motivates what we do in life:

Power

Selflessness

Money

Passion

Love

Next Promotion

Deadline

Lifestyle

Opposition

Fame

Competition

Mastery

Impact

Be the best

Social media

Patrick Bet-David, founder of Valuetainment, claims that the motivations of man are inexhaustible, and this is somewhat true, as almost anything can drive a man.

Some people are driven by power. Here, they always want to be in charge. There's a voracious craving for winning, and when such people lose, they tend to break down. This drive is common amongst folks who are obsessed with winning, and nothing satisfies them in the first place. In the same vein, some folks are driven by a strong yearning for recognition. Here, such folks want to prove they are right, and others are wrong. People like Lee Iacocca are driven by the need to be recognized. History has it that after he was fired by Ford Motors, he went on to join Chrysler, another automobile company. He led the company out of debt and transformed it into a massive company, and he was recognized by all and sundry.

Tom Watson also had a similar story. He used to work for a tech company called NCR. There, he was fired, and he was determined to prove his former boss wrong. Tom joined another start-up, CTR. The start-up grew to become one of the leading technology companies in the world, the International Business Machines Corporation. And yes, he did prove his boss wrong. So, you can see that our motivations play a vital role in the results our life produces. They define the kind of person we are, the value system we hold, and the virtues we possess. It is a subtle realization, yet as powerful as a blow from Muhammed Ali himself.

Another thing that motivates our actions in life is money. It has become the major influence of this century and has inspired many folks to work hard at their jobs, even if they don't feel fulfilled working those jobs.

I have met folks whose primary drive is money; it gingers them. Well, this is not bad in and of itself, but most folks that follow this path have a higher chance of becoming depressed.

The truth is, it makes a lot of short-term sense to be driven by money; trust me, being broke is not a good thing. The danger is when it becomes the operating system that runs our life.

The other day, Adekunle Gold, a popular Nigerian highlife singer, took to his Twitter and posted:

> *Money no dey bring happiness*
>
> *Na when I get the money I realize*
>
> *But I no be hypocrite*
>
> *I dey pray make you get your own too*

Although, here I believe the artiste is talking about fulfilment and not happiness. There's a big difference between fulfilment and happiness, and this understanding will help us in picking the right motivations for our life. And this is something I call 'drawing from the spring within'.

HOW TO DRAW FROM THE SPRING WITHIN (INTRINSIC MOTIVATION)

Categorically, motivations can be classified into two: intrinsic and extrinsic motivations. Let's start with the latter.

With extrinsic motivation, here, rewards and incentives play a major role. Do you know you experience a surge of energy when someone promises to give you a gift for completing a task?

Or when your boss promises you a raise for completing a task? It helps you hustle to get that prize, and this is exactly what extrinsic motivation is. As I mentioned earlier, motivations like recognition, fame, and money are external. Anything that motivates a person and comes from an external element is extrinsic motivation. Understanding this will help you define the things that motivate you and help you pick the right motivations.

When a person is externally motivated, it means they do not consider inner fulfilment for the sake of inner fulfilment; it's not something we want to do – we do it to gain a reward or avoid a punishment. Such actions, decisions, or tasks become more of an obligation than an activity that will bring you enjoyment or fulfilment.

External motivation is common; like air, it is everywhere. It is responsible for the rise of internet fraudsters, folks living fake lives… the list is endless. This kind of motivation does not lead to a successful life, and most folks who follow this path live in the shadows of others, doing the things they do not believe in just for a reward or incentives. This kind of motivation can be seductive; fine, honest men have played Judas, and many times swept integrity under the carpet.

I'll be biased and say nothing good comes out of being externally motivated. Certainly, there is *some* good, like the stories of IBM and Chrysler I narrated earlier. You can still make magic with external motivations, rise to the highest rank at your job, prove the world wrong and mayhap become the president of the United States of

America. That's beautiful, right? The problem is this package does not come with a guarantee – the guarantee of fulfilment. And this is because it was not really about you in the first place. Well, you could argue that it was everything you wanted, but in a few years, would you feel fulfilled?

And please don't mistake happiness for fulfilment; they are different. Simon Sinek says it better: "Fulfilment is not another word for happiness. All kinds of things make us happy at work: hitting a goal, getting a promotion, landing a new client, completing a project – the list goes on. But happiness is temporary; the feeling doesn't last. Nobody walks around energized by the memory of a goal hit twelve years ago. That intensity passes with time."

Now read this carefully:

> *Fulfilment is deeper. Fulfilment lasts. The difference between happiness and fulfilment is the difference between liking and loving something. We don't necessarily like our kids all the time, but we do love them all the time. We don't necessarily find happiness in our jobs every day, but we can feel fulfilled by our work every day if it makes us feel part of something bigger than ourselves.*

Does this resonate with you?

This is the reason we can feel unfulfilled even if we are successful by standard measures like compensation, status, money, or what people would say. Happiness comes from what we do, while fulfilment comes from why we do it, and if the reason we do what we do is external, then there is a high chance that we may never know fulfilment.

Now, the stage is set. Let's talk about the spring within (intrinsic motivation).

Intrinsic motivation can be defined as the elements responsible for the actions we take without any obvious rewards. Here, we are driven by internal reward, and most times, this is naturally satisfying. We simply enjoy the process or perceive it to be an opportunity for us to learn, grow, and maximize our ability.

For example, what are the things you do for the love of it? No rewards, no incentives – just pure passion and interest. The keyword here is PASSION. It is an off-shoot of the spring within, the inner force that guides us to fulfilment.

Simply put, when your decisions are fuelled by internal desires, away from any reward system or incentives, you will move beyond happiness into fulfilment. The good thing about intrinsic motivators is that they are healthy for us. They build good habits in us and help us give our 100% wherever we find ourselves.

Jay-Jay Okocha, while he was playing at Bolton Wanderers, made a profound statement in a post-match interview; he said, "Anywhere I find myself, I give my best." This statement shows passion and a level of intrinsic motivation. And yes, he got paid well. Don't think you can't get rewarded for passion – you can. But doing a thing solely because of reward would, over time, make you incentive-sensitive and reduce your ground-level productivity.

Let your motivation come from the spring within you because this is the only spring that can never dry up. External motivations are dependent on other variables and not you. You have control over the spring inside of you; let that be your driving force.

IN THE VALLEY OF DECISION

Whenever you see a successful business, someone once made a courageous decision. – Peter F. Drucker
When one can accept that all their circumstances and life events are a result of their decision making, that individual immediately gains back their power to create. – Michael Austin Jacobs

Decision-making is a sensitive and important aspect of human life. In our day-to-day lives, we have to make decisions. Some of these decisions vary in magnitude. From little decisions to significant decisions, every stage of our life is littered with choices. And the decisions that we make have a significant influence on our lives. That is why the process of decision-making is an important one.

Some decisions may seem easy to reach, while others are complex, but how right the choices we make are and how timely they are is what matters. This will greatly determine their impact. Some of the decisions that we make include personal decisions, business-related, career decisions, political decisions, and decisions about our relationships or love life. All these decisions are influenced by many factors. The important thing, however, is for one to be keen before reaching decisions. This is the only way that you can be sure of making decisions that you will not regret in the future. In this chapter, we'll look at certain models we can apply when making decisions and I'm persuaded that these models could change your life.

Firstly, I want you to know that our life is a result of the choices and decisions we make, regardless of how trivial or minute these decisions might seem. In a simple sense, decision-making is the act of choosing between two or more courses of action. Have you read a memoir or watched one? Here, the subject's life is analysed, and one can see how crucial the most trivial decisions can be and how they can influence a person's life.

I once read *Hard Choices Poem* by Jojoba Mansell:

> *A path is laid out ahead,*
>
> *It forks before your feet.*
>
> *A decision filled with dread,*
>
> *Uncertain of what you'll meet.*

A game full of chance,

Of many hidden pitfalls.

To find true romance,

Dare you risk losing all?

Choices never easy to make,

Fog seems to cloud your way.

You fear making a mistake,

Of gambling and losing the day.

But life is full of Hard Choices,

And the risk is part of the game.

Be brave, ignore doubting voices,

Make the choice, life won't be the same.

My favourite line in this poem is: "choices never easy to make." I find resonance with that. One of the hardest things to do in life is to make a good decision, not just responding to pressure or impulse but to make a sound and accurate decision. And one way to analyse your decisions, to make the best of the choices you have, is through what is called 'delayed gratification'.

Before we talk about delayed gratification, let's examine what is called the 'marshmallow experiment', as this will aid our understanding of delayed gratification.

The marshmallow experiment

This experiment took place in the 1960s. Children were brought into a closed room, and a researcher sat each child in a chair and placed a marshmallow on the table. Now, a marshmallow is a type of confectionery that is made from sugar, water, and gelatin, whipped to a solid but has a soft feel. Think of it as a ball of cake, and you know how much children love cake, right?

The researcher made a deal with them: "I'm leaving the room now. If you don't eat this ball of cake while I'm away, I'll reward you with a second marshmallow. However, if you decide to eat this marshmallow before I come back, then there will be no second marshmallow for you." At this point, the researcher offered a deal to the child and said, "Do you understand?" The children nodded in affirmation.

The choice before them was quite simple: one ball of cake right now or two balls later. The researcher left the room for about 15 minutes.

And as you can imagine, watching the children wait in the room was interesting viewing; some of the kids jumped up and ate the first marshmallow as soon as the researcher closed the door. Others were pacing, bouncing, or scooting in their chairs as they tried to resist the temptation. Perhaps they were saying, "A child shall not live by marshmallow alone," but eventually they gave in to temptation. And finally, a few of the children did manage to wait the entire time; they waited for the second marshmallow. This is the basis of delayed gratification.

Delayed gratification can be defined as the discipline of resisting an impulse for an immediately available reward in the hope of obtaining a more valued reward in the future. This trait is common among successful people; they always look at the bigger picture and wait for the second marshmallow. Your ability to delay gratification is crucial to self-control and to making good decisions.

This principle is universal. Look around, you'll see this playing out almost everywhere. For example, if you delay the gratification of watching television and get your homework done now, then you'll learn more and get better grades. In this same vein, if you delay the gratification of buying desserts and chips at the store, then you'll eat healthier when you get home. Or if you delay the gratification of finishing your workout early and put in a few more reps, then you'll be stronger. You see the pattern, right?

James Clear, the author of *Atomic Habits*, puts it this way: "Success usually comes down to choosing the pain of discipline over the ease of distraction. And that's exactly what delayed gratification is all about." You have to wait for the checkmate and not take the queen off the board. In the game of chess, the goal is to checkmate – to put the king in a position that it can move to any other square. Amateur chess players fall for the trap of taking other pieces, the queen especially, instead of focusing on checkmate.

Another reason you should always apply delayed gratification is because it instils patience and endurance, and you won't lose out on the main thing. It's tempting to settle for the pleasure of the moment, and that's understandable. Pleasure is important to our survival. We'll always need things like food, water, and shelter to survive and enjoy our time here. Regardless, as we get older and mature, it is crucial that we learn to tolerate the discomfort of delayed gratification if we have a greater purpose or goal in mind, a life worth living. In all the decisions you make in your life, endeavour to keep delayed gratification as a model in your mind; always consider it before you make your move.

Let's look at another model you can use or consider when making decisions – Thinking in the Long Term.

Have you ever heard of 'long-term thinking'?

In psychology, long-term thinking involves an intentional consideration of what might happen in the future, what our choices for affecting the future are, and what we know or do not know about the consequences of those choices. And all of these considerations must be part of building a better future. So, you must pay attention to the effect or results of this decision in the future. Time travel in your mind and examine your choices. You should also critically analyse all the properties of your choices; don't get carried away by rewards or incentives.

Long-term thinking requires us to break free from uncertainty, and most times, this serves as a blockage to our creativity. We must look beyond the current state of affairs, and instead, keep our minds open to what is possible, even if the possibility seems remote today.

Although, thinking about what might happen also requires us to allow space for uncertainty and surprise. Life is not all 1's and 0's. Even as intelligent as humans have grown over thousands of years, we still can't predict the future. We still don't fully understand how earth systems work, and the bodies we carry still carry mysteries we have yet to understand. And they are even harder to predict. Both the earth and the human body are full of surprises.

Futurist Wendy Schultz said it well: "While the future is uncertain and much of it is beyond our control, we can control many aspects of it. We choose our future: we create it by what we do or fail to do."

The future cannot be predetermined. The world is a mix of the predictable and the unpredictable, the things we can't choose, and the things we can. Long-term thinking helps us navigate our way in between all of this and helps us avoid regrets.

Regarding regret, there's something called the Regret Minimization Framework. It's a really simple model. It all starts with a question: In X years, will I regret taking this decision? It's also similar to long-term thinking. Jeff Bezos had an idea. A great idea. But he hadn't made the jump yet. He was not too certain. So, he thought about it for a while and decided. He said, "I knew that when I was 80, I was not going to regret having tried this. I was not going to regret trying to participate in this thing called the Internet that I thought was going to be a really big deal. I knew that if I failed, I wouldn't regret that, but I knew the one thing I might regret is not ever having tried."

It's really simple yet powerful. At least, it made Jeff Bezos the richest man in the world. You too can make so much progress in decision-making if you apply this.

There is another problem-solving strategy that you can also apply in making decisions. It goes like this:

"If you're stuck, shift up a level or two (think bigger picture) or down a level or two (think finer details). Many problems are solvable at different levels."

This works for decision-making too. You'll often find better choices at different levels of your life. The truth is, life is filled with choices and those choices are choices that affect us both every day and in everything we do, which means choices are not without significance. What we choose to do does not only affect us, but it also affects others, whether we see the results immediately or not. What is a decision? It is to settle, determine, or bring to a resolution; or, in other words, to decide or to make up one's mind. Decisions can either make us or mar us. Decisions can either paddle us in the right direction if we are in the same boat with the right person or take us to the wrong destination.

People often say that they find it hard to make decisions. Unfortunately, we all have to make decisions all the time, ranging from trivial issues like what to have for lunch, right up to life-changing decisions like where and what to study, and whom to marry. Some people put off making decisions by endlessly searching for more information or getting other people to offer their recommendations. Others resort to decision-making by taking a vote, sticking a pin in a list, or tossing a coin.

Herbert Simon said, and I agree with him that decision or decision making "is a matter of compromise." Why is it so? Before a policy/decision-maker, there are several decisions, and while making a decision, he is to select one or more alternatives that will be suitable for him or will serve his purpose.

It is said that Herbert Simon is a pioneer in the field of decision-making concepts because he felt that if a decision was not taken properly and timely, it may spoil the objective of the business organization; keeping this in mind, it is essential that an organization resort to utmost caution as to the adoption of the decision, and at the same time, will focus on the implementation of the decision. So, both taking and implementing decisions is important.

This is the conclusion: Think in the long term, delay gratification, consider if you might regret your choices, and everything else will fall into place.

Chapter Seven

TAMING YOUR FOXES

Make no mistake about it. Bad habits are called 'bad' for a reason. They kill our productivity and creativity. They slow us down. They hold us back from achieving our goals. And they're detrimental to our health. – John Rampton

The story of one of R&B's greatest, R. Kelly, is one that drives me to deep reflection every time it comes to mind. A talented and fulfilled singer and producer, his award-laden career was brought to an inglorious end in 2019 in the wake of multiple sexual allegations against him. Those accusations weren't new; the songwriter had faced accusations of sexual predation of young girls since the start of his career. However, he met his waterloo in 2019 after the release of a documentary where his victims spoke up. His bad habits dug the grave that will bury his glorious career.

R. Kelly isn't the only great man whose glorious career has been buried under the rubble of bad habits. We can name more than a few successful people who have met a pitiful end because of one bad habit or another. It is as though bad habits wait till one gets to the peak of one's career before making a mess of things.

And we are not immune to bad habits either. Some of us are still afloat because we have yet to reach a point in our career where a little mistake stemming from bad behaviour can make it all come crashing down.

***

One of my favourite phrases in the Bible is from the *Songs of Solomon*: "Catch the foxes for us, the little foxes that spoil the vineyards, for our vineyards are in blossom." This phrase has helped me pay more attention to my inadequacies and deal with them. In this chapter, we'll talk about how you can identify your weaknesses and how you can deal with them. Here, there won't be a set of rules, rather I'll be using certain narratives to guide you through. Kindly pay attention, as this will transform your life.

HOW TO IDENTIFY YOUR WEAKNESSES (THE THINGS THAT BREAKS US)

I once read a psychoanalytic review of the life of Richard Nixon, former president of the United States of America. He was impeached for what is known as the 'Watergate scandal'. The summary of the scandal is this: the former president tried to cover up a burglary at the Democratic National Committee (DNC) headquarters; it was said that the building was also wiretapped illegally. I don't want to bore you with the politics, but the keyword here is 'cover-up'. He tried to cover up a crime.

According to David Abrahamsen, the author of *Nixon vs Nixon: An emotional tragedy*, Nixon had been involved in a burglary way back when he was in boarding school. He and his friends were too eager to see their results; they couldn't wait for Monday morning. The thing is – Nixon was not caught at this time. Perhaps this, and other atrocities he committed growing up, made him think he could get away with anything. Nixon was once quoted saying, "If the president does it, then it is not crooked."

But this is the thing with our weaknesses: they eventually grow into the very thing that breaks us.

The first step to identifying the things that break us is what I call 'sincere sincerity'.

Some of us have recurring habits in our lives, and these things drag us from a dazzling, wealthy state of mind to the direst poverty – in character and our entire wellbeing. The problem with most of us is that we make excuses for ourselves. Kindly note that whatever you make excuses for consistently is a weakness; never forget this. You have to be completely sincere with yourself to pinpoint the behaviours you are prone to. This process begins with identifying simple things, like eating too much or oversleeping, to more complex things, like low self-esteem, anger, distractions, and cognitive dissonance.

The truth is, you can have all these things and still play Judas. For instance, I used to have a friend, Daniel, who had an issue with his temper. His friends always complained about it, but he kept brushing them off. So, on his birthday, he had a small party, and everything went well until the anchor of the party asked, "Who has anything to say about Daniel?" Three people ended with the same note: "He has anger issues."

There are a lot of folks who are exactly like Daniel; they turn a blind eye to their weaknesses. Then, all of a sudden, it explodes before their eyes. You can prevent this in your own life, and all it would take is your 'sincere sincerity'. The good thing is that sincerity will open your eyes to every bad habit and weakness, and like light, it will light up every shadow.

Another virtue that can help you identify your weaknesses before they grow into the things that break you is pay attention to details. John Wooden once said, "It's the little details that are vital. Little things make big things happen." And this is true. If you pay close attention to the minutest bit of your character and attitudes, and with the goggles of sincerity, you'll see the recurring pattern.

Let me tell you about my friend, Benjamin. Growing up, he was always afraid of failing. The teacher once caught him cheating in the examination hall, and his excuse was that he felt he had not read enough for the paper. Many years later, instead of pursuing a career in writing,

Benjamin took a job at a bank. Although he hated banking, he was too afraid to follow his passion. For Benjamin, fear was a prominent weakness, and so far, it has led him to live in bondage and unfulfillment. Beyond adding to your resume that you pay attention to details, apply this basic principle to your life and you will make so much progress. Please don't fall into the delusion of people that believe they do not have weaknesses; please don't. This has ignorantly robbed many of time to seek early solutions and help. Always check yourself, your motives, your motivations; always keep an eye out for your flaws and improve on them.

Another process that can help you identify your weakness is journaling.

Journaling is a written record of our thoughts and feelings. Mina Murray says it better: "Journaling is like whispering to oneself and listening at the same time."

The good thing about journaling is that it allows you to track patterns in your life, and if you pay close attention to these patterns, you will be able to sift out your weaknesses.

Other benefits of journaling include:

Managing anxiety

Reducing stress

Coping with depression

And it helps you prioritize your problems and fears.

Tracking your problems daily helps to see your triggers as well as how to be aware of them and solve them more effectively.

Journaling also helps to identify negative thoughts and behaviours. It allows us to see our problems with more clarity and helps us develop a new perspective on things that are happening daily in our life. It also fosters self-discovery.

HOW TO DEAL WITH YOUR WEAKNESS (TAMING YOUR FOXES)

We all have weaknesses that limit us – little foxes that spoil our vineyard. That thing you swore not to do again, yet you still find yourself doing it – yes, I know the feeling. Without any controversy, if we are to achieve anything great in life – rise to stardom without falling, become exceptional leaders, and live a peaceful and fulfilling life – we must deal with our weaknesses. And this involves taking the pieces of our life and charging forward in the right direction.

The rules for dealing with our weaknesses are not set in stone, so there's no one way to do it. Yet, the result is the same – the fox must be tamed. And this is because weaknesses left untended to or ignored can lead to great mishaps. When we focus on our strengths and neglect our weaknesses, it shows that we are building on our opportunities rather than solving our problems. And as is one of the cruel ways of nature, problems left unattended do not go away, and they, often times, escalate.

Our weaknesses are usually qualified with negative adjectives, such as: lethargic, aggressive, slow-willed, irresponsible, mistrustful, rude, shy, etc. And as much as these words sound scary and tough, believe me, they aren't that powerful when you identify them and deal with them.

Sometimes, dealing with your weakness means you can convert them into weapons for use. For instance, a person who has issues with shyness could find out that being shy is sometimes the saving grace you need to get out of a tight position. A shy person, however, just needs to be a good evaluator and identify when being shy is a weakness.

Another case is being slow. You can work around this habit by using it as a model in making decisions; use it to learn the virtue of patience. This comes in handy in some situations where patience is required before taking certain steps. Likewise, a slow-willed person will, often times, think matters through before arriving at a decision. The issue is striking a balance; you must know when to wait and when not to.

Here are two key strategies you can easily remember when you want to deal with a weakness:

CREATE A PLAN

After identifying your weakness, you need to create a plan for yourself to address it. You are not looking for a quick fix; you want to permanently fix it. What are you going to do to follow through? What are the triggers? How do you want to avoid those?

If you are serious about overcoming your weaknesses, then you must come up with a viable plan. You're probably curious about how to create a plan. Well, your plan must include the following:

What is the weakness?

What are the triggers?

How to avoid the triggers?

Accountability

If you are not certain you can do this on your own, let's move to the second strategy:

SEEK SUPPORT

There are people out there willing to listen and lend a helping hand whenever you reach out. They are there to help you walk through the pain and overcome that which has held you back for much of your life. There are people out there who have been through similar situations and learned how to overcome their fears and weaknesses. Seek their help. Ask for their support. We are often too afraid to reach out. We are too afraid to reveal the truth to others. But don't be. Don't allow your ego to shroud the truth one moment longer. If your reasons for wanting to overcome those limiting things in your life are strong enough, you'll reach out right now.

It's okay to be scared. It's okay to be afraid. But it's not okay to continue to suffer the mental or emotional torment for one moment longer. No, you have to seek the help and support of others – personally or professionally. There's absolutely nothing wrong with it. You're human. You're fallible. No one is perfect. No one.

Chapter Eight

SWIMMING THROUGH THE CURRENTS

If you meet the darkest moment of life, strive valiantly through it with courage and never retreat, for you shall surely meet light afterward. If you meet the muddy stream of life, swim across it with the tenacity to the very end for there is a clearer stream that shall wash your dirt away afterward. If all people reject you in the mid of the arduous race of life, dare to smile and move on for there are people who await you to embrace you in the end.
– Ernest Agyemang Yeboah

Bayern Munich star player and Champions League winner, Alphonso Davies, was born in a refugee camp in Ghana in the year 2000. During this time, Liberia was in a civil war, his parents had to flee, and as destiny would have it, he found himself in the land of freedom and justice. He stayed there for five years before his parents moved to Canada as immigrants. Today, Davies has risen to stardom. But this did not come easily;

he had to deal with racists from Vancouver Whitecaps youth in 2015 at the age of 14. Even now at Bayern, he still has these issues. And when we talk about racism, we are talking about a psychological attack on a person because of their skin colour or where they hail from.

For instance, Mesut Özil, a star of the German national soccer team and one of the most expensive German players in the sport's history, resigned from playing for his national team because of this same issue – racism. Now, imagine what it would have felt like for Davies, at the age of 14, to be tossed around, spoken to rudely, and perhaps sometimes even beaten up. And yet, amidst it all, he didn't give up on his dream.

The truth is that there will always be one storm or another to weather in life. Life is not just a smooth, untroubled sea where we have a jolly good ride, no. As much as the thought of a life without trials and tribulation is appealing, life is not designed that way. If so, there wouldn't be victors and victims.

Like a road, life has many bends, ups, and downs, but that's the beauty of it. One day, you might feel as if you have it all planned out and things are working out just fine. However, the next day, you are appalled by the emptiness that is your life. You seemed cocooned in chaos and depression, and you don't know how to forge ahead. That is the paradox of our lives. And it is in swimming through these currents of trials and tribulations, weathering the storms of failure and depression, that our character is refined, and our victory is born.

The problem with a lot of us is that we do not possess the grit to get back up every time life kicks us down. We lack resolve, and when the tiniest of storms hit us, we melt under the weight of self-pity and defeat.

The great Michael Jordan once said, "I've missed more than 9000 shots in my career. I've lost almost 300 games. 26 times, I've been trusted to take the game-winning shot and missed. I've failed over and over and over again in my life and that is why I succeed." I want you to see that challenges are part of the process; they are unavoidable.

Look at the challenges, problems, and difficult issues in your life as crucial phases in which you will gather the experiences necessary to help you become wiser and stronger. Challenges mould and shape us.

Again, don't be part of the class of people who fantasize about a life without problems. They only want to enjoy the goodies of life, take in the beautiful scenery of Maldives, wear bespoke fashion styles, and have everything breath-taking. Well, this is an impossible goal. We all have problems in this life, whether big or small; challenges are inevitable.

Let's try a simple exercise: Put your hand on your chest and say, "I accept that there will be challenges in my life, but they won't crumble me. I will overcome." Although this may seem stupid to you, what you are doing is subtly installing a mindset that accepts the challenges of life and overcomes them.

So don't run away from the problems and challenges you are facing in life. Don't ignore them or try to hide from them. Face them. Deal with them. The greatest growth in life and the most important lessons you are to learn will come when you face a serious challenge or problem and deal with it. Regardless of the result, value the experience and personal growth, and you'll make tremendous progress in your life.

HOW TO OVERCOME THE CHALLENGES OF LIFE

One thing I have to realize about life is that it takes continuous effort to overcome the challenges that come our way. Sometimes, it looks like the universe is designed in such a way that every day comes with new hurdles, and you always have to be on guard to overcome these hurdles. In case you are already feeling weary and thinking of giving up, you should read this section with the utmost attention. I believe it will give you the right boost of energy to push through.

CHANGE YOUR PERSPECTIVE

The first thing challenging situations do to us is affect our perspectives. Let's say you woke up to an email complaint from your boss that said you made a huge mistake on a project, and you have to work through the weekend. This means all your plans to get away with your friends have to be called off. If you are not careful, the rest of your day will go in the wrong direction. Most people would allow this to affect their state of mind; they become moody and engage the rest of their day with negativity. Never allow a challenge to change your perspective to the negative. Instead of reacting, respond instead.

From the moment you read the email, you should reflect on how to solve the problem. Don't be a person who complains instead of looking for solutions. You should make it a habit to never let negativity take over. I'm not saying you should force yourself to be positive, but at least try to keep a positive perspective on challenges. Think of responding and not reacting; think of solutions and not complaints. The truth is, if you let your energy go to waste on reacting and complaining, you'll be drained of energy before you even begin to figure out how to overcome your challenges.

ASK THE RIGHT QUESTIONS

When life gets difficult, it is very easy to focus on the things that are not working. And most times, this eventually leads to depressing thoughts. Instead of wallowing in thoughts that give you negative energy, asking *Why did this happen to me?*, take a chill pill and answer the question: If the challenges you have faced so far in your life did not happen to you, do you think you would be as strong and wise as you are today? I am guessing not. So, instead of asking *why me*, ask: What is responsible for this challenge? Why did it happen? How can I solve this? And more importantly: What can I learn from it?

Remember – for every challenge you overcome, you must be able to pinpoint the lesson you learned from it such that if it occurs again, you won't be caught unaware.

SEEK SUPPORT

In the previous chapter, we talked about how reaching out helps in dealing with our weaknesses; we can also use the same model when dealing with our challenges. You know your weaknesses are also a kind of challenge, right?

You came into this world alone, and you'll leave alone. Yet, every human depends on others for their survival. Even the strongest economies in the world are interdependent. It's on you to reach out for help when you are emotionally or physically strained. Sometimes, after several attempts to proffer a solution without making any headway, you should go ahead and seek out support or help. A third party will likely be able to offer a perspective you hadn't seen. The truth is, having someone to support you through your tough time is great. The best scenario is when they have the expertise to get you over the hurdle. Even if that's not the case, the emotional support is more than enough to keep you going in tough times. They may also be able to present examples of challenges you have overcome to motivate you to overcome whatever it is you are facing now.

***

You have to understand that winning does not come easily; no one makes great achievements on the first day. World-famous cricket player Sachin Tendulkar did not become popular in one day. It took him overcoming many failures and challenges to become what he is today. When he faced failure, he did not give up; he kept trying till he met success in life. Similarly, when we face challenges in our own life, we should not give in to them. Always remember that you may not be responsible for the challenges that are happening in your life; it could be something that is completely outside your control. But you are responsible for the actions you take. If you act like a victim – blaming others, reacting, complaining, and not taking responsibility for your life – nothing will change about your life.

Let me leave you with this short essay I found on the internet, *The secret of those achievers by Vijit Malviya;* it ministered to me, and I'm persuaded it will do the same to you:

> *How many of us have succeeded in what we try in the first attempt? Not many. This proves that success cannot be attained in one day. There are exceptions where success can be achieved easily. But when it comes to a competitive task or a tough task it takes a lot of patience and needs many attempts to bring success to our side.*
>
> *We would have heard about the great scientist Thomas Alva Edison. His success story is motivating. Edison in his experiments to refine the light bulb failed 1000 times. But his attitude towards failure was simply great. He confidently said, "I didn't fail 1,000 times. I found 1000 ways of how not to make a light bulb."*

In life, what matters is our attitude. If we give up easily, we cannot taste the flavour of success. It takes years for a tree to give a tasty fruit. Similarly, it will take time to make success, sometimes even years. The path of success can be rough and hard, but if we keep going without any lack of confidence the day to success is not far away. If we want to win in life we should not stop till we get what we are looking for.

What will help us mark achievements is self-confidence. If we believe we can make wonders, we will. So, we should believe ourselves before expecting others to believe us or support us.

When life gives us a thousand reasons to quit trying, give yourself one reason to try one more time. "Never Give Up" till you become a great achiever.

Hey, the next time you face a challenge, don't give in. And if you are currently facing a challenge, don't give up.

Chapter Nine

CLIMBING THE GIANT'S SHOULDERS

*If I have seen further, it is by standing on the
shoulders of giants. – Isaac Newton*

At 19, Deshauna Barber could never have
thought of becoming Miss USA. In fact, while
working part-time in a US store, Target, it never
crossed her mind. Leslie Morton, a former Miss
Texas contestant, was the miracle that happened
to her. She was hell-bent on pushing Deshauna
to the regional pageant.

Wait.

Brace yourself for a shocker. Are you ready?

Here it goes…

Deshauna failed six times straight in six
years. She did not qualify for the regionals, yet

Leslie did not give up on her. Little wonder Deshauana's favourite quote is "Do not fear failure"; God knows she had had her taste of it. In this dark moment of her life, she was not alone. Leslie kept telling her, *Keep trying, you'll get it* – and she did. Deshauna got it.

The role of mentorship cannot be overemphasised. Most times, mentors are the bridge between where we are and where we are going. They help cut down the long process towards our goal, minimizing the number of our failures because we get to learn from their lived experience and the wisdom gathered from it.

You see, think of mentorship as a relationship between two parties, where party A has more experience, knowledge, and connections, and is able to pass along what they have learned to party B, who is a junior in the given field. Mentorship involves the sharing of information, emotional support, and guidance from someone with experience to someone in need of that experience.

If you look at the most successful people today, you'll see that they stood on the shoulders of those that have gone before them. For instance, Tim Cook, the CEO of Apple, after taking over from the phenomenal Steve Jobs, had a hard time going about his new role. But he was not alone; he had always looked up to Steve Jobs as a mentor. So, Jobs helped him, taught him, and well, reduced the friction Cook would have faced alone had he not had guidance.

Google's CEO, Larry Page, has had many people whom he has called his mentor over the years. Like Cook, Jobs too was someone Page sought advice from, but probably the mentor he credits for much of his and Sergey Brin's success, particularly during the early years of their company, was Rajeev Motwani. Later on in their career, they brought on Eric Schmidt to help them build the corporate infrastructure needed for Google to become the second biggest company in the world. Warren Buffett had Benjamin Graham as his mentor; Jeff Bezos had David Shaw; Howard Schultz, the CEO of Starbucks, had Warren Bennis as his mentor. All these are prominent men who have risen to stardom. They did not rise by their wits alone; they had someone holding their hand. And today, the rest is history. We hear their name, read about them in the news; most of them have a foundation in mentorship.

WHY YOU NEED A MENTOR

Mentorship has its origins as far back as ancient Greece. Back then, it was used as a tool to impart young men and women with important virtues. It then developed into a craftsman or apprentice relationship. Here, a young person learns a craft by observing his master. Mentorship also grew into a development strategy, especially in a career. Here, an expert in a particular field shares his experience with juniors in the field. So, you see this thing called 'mentorship' did not start yesterday. Hence, having established this, the following are reasons you need a mentor:

INFORMATION AND KNOWLEDGE

In a mentorship relationship, mentors provide information and knowledge to their mentees. As

Benjamin Franklin once said, "Tell me and I forget; teach me and I may remember; involve me and I learn."

In the same vein, mentors can see where we need to improve when we often cannot. A famous movie maker, George Lucas, says, "Mentors have a way of seeing more of our faults than we would like. It's the only way we grow."

One of the amazing things about having a mentor is they will always be brutally honest with you and tell you exactly how it is rather than downplay any weaknesses they see in you. Ever heard of constructive criticism? Well, it is the art of offering valid and well-reasoned opinions about the work of others, usually involving both positive and negative comments, in a friendly manner rather than in an oppositional one. Mentors consistently engage this in bringing the best out of you. I used to have a friend back in high school who loved writing; he worked on his craft day and night and was known in school as an amazing writer. Some of the other guys called him William Shakespeare. Then he submitted an entry for a popular magazine. He could not believe the review he got. Well, that changed everything for him. He reached out to the English teacher for help, and this improved his craft tremendously. The problem with some of us is we have ego issues. We don't enjoy being criticized, even if it's for our good. Don't be that person who despises constructive criticism. Accept it and you'll make so much progress.

GROWTH

Mentors help us grow professionally and personally. Steven Spielberg, the famous movie director, once said, "The delicate balance of mentoring someone is not creating them in your image, but allowing them to create themselves." Mentors serve as catalysts for growth; they push you hard to bring out the best in you. This does not mean that you cannot grow without a mentor – you can. But the rate of your growth will be slow because you will learn a lot of things the hard way. You don't want that, trust me.

MENTORS HELP YOU FIND YOURSELF

Oprah Winfrey once said, "A mentor is someone who allows you to see inside of yourself." I understand that there are a million ways to self-discovery and finding the light inside of you. I dare say that mentorship makes it easier. Think of a mentor as a shepherd that keeps a sheep till it becomes fat and ready for stew. Please note that having a mentor is not a sign of weakness; it shows you are smart enough and are driven enough to succeed. It also shows that you don't want to waste time walking in the dark. Life can be a pint easier with mentorship.

You see, having a mentor can help you find time and transform your vision.

They provide ideas, thoughts, and insights that challenge and enable you to see beyond your sphere of influence. Mentors can amplify your vision by elevating your thinking capabilities; they'll help you connect the dots and see patterns.

Having a mentor can transform your life, elevating you by making their shoulders your platform. They prop you up, and this demonstration of trust should not be abused as their extensions are a critical validation that will eventually open doors and grant you access to opportunities beyond your circle.

HOW TO FIND AND RETAIN A MENTOR

1. Find someone you want to be like

Jeff Goins wrote: "Don't just find someone who has a job you want or a platform that you covet. Find someone that is like you, someone with a similar set of strengths and skills you want to emulate. Otherwise, you'll just end up frustrated. Spend some time finding the right person. In fact, have several candidates before committing to a single mentor."

It is needful to add that finding a mentor you want to be like is easier when you have a mental picture of who you want to be. Of course, you might not grasp the full picture yet as clarity is a thing we gain as we progress in knowledge and in understanding ourselves and our purpose, but having a mental picture of who you want to be will help you in finding who you want to be like.

2. Study the person

It is not enough to find the person you want to be like; you have to study them too. And you don't need to know them up close before you do this, although closeness is a tremendous advantage. You should buy their books and materials, follow their social media pages and blog, if they have one. This will give you insight into their thought process and help reshape yours as well. It will also give you a ready template to follow.

3. Form a relationship

Now that you have found the person you want to be like, and you have laid hold of their materials, the next thing to do is try and form a relationship with them. It is not always advisable to ask them to be your mentor, even though you can do that. But, at times, you form a relationship by being visible – not by stalking, but by being visible to them. Volunteer for their causes and comment on their posts, for example, until you build enough visibility to ask for their mentorship.

4. Don't force the relationship

Mentor relationships should not be forced. Instead, they should be allowed to grow organically.

You must understand that what your mentor is giving you is the gift of their time, and time is expensive. So, instead of always asking for one-on-one meetings with them, learn to get information through observation. Observe them, their process, and how they get things done; then you can ask questions regarding those aspects that you need proper clarity in.

5. Don't be a pest

Some people approach mentorship with a pest mentality. They only want to take and take, to always be at the receiving end and never give. This is morally wrong. A mentorship relationship should be symbiotic. They are giving you their time, and you have to pay with your service, respect, and honour.

6. Commit to the relationship

A lot of people back down from a mentor relationship because they are not receptive to criticism and correction, even when it is constructive. Also, they are too lazy to be invested in it, to meet with the demands it comes with, and so they quit the relationship when criticism comes and when the demands become too much for them. By doing this, however, they deny themselves from reaping the benefits of the relationship. These are people who become half-baked, never fully committing to a process in their lives.

7. Respect and honour

Two things must be constant in your relationship with your mentor, and those are respect and honour. These two elements are essential if you are to gain from the relationship. For one, when you respect and honour your mentor, they, in turn, will see the need to commit to you. This will also help you avoid the trap of overfamiliarity. One of the things that kills any form of relationship is overfamiliarity, and having a posture of respect and honour will help you avoid that trap.

***

Whatever you want to do in life, having a mentor is essential. It is not that mentors make your journey entirely easy; they could, but most, essentially, will help you avoid familiar pitfalls on your road to success.

To see far in life, you have to stand on the shoulders of giants. Giants have gone through the process; they have completed or gone far in the journey you have just begun, and as such, their life, experience, and wisdom become a template for you in charting your own course.

Chapter Ten

STAYING TRUE

Life does not respond to pity, it responds to principles. – Deji Ajibade

What I set out to do in this book is to give light to certain existential questions, such as: Why are we unhappy? What are the things that matter? Much more, I proffer principles I believe will help you achieve wholesome living. These principles are essential because life does not respond to pity, it responds to principles. Our universe is based on order, and this truth is established by reason of the various laws that govern our world.

In the first chapter we talk about unhappiness – the reason we are unhappy, why we walk through the corridors of depression and struggle to live a fulfilling life.

In chapter two, I talked about the 'more' trap and why we are stuck in the cycle of wanting more. This, I would like to reiterate, is not an argument against wanting the good things in life; instead, it points to the need for us to strike the balance between ambition and contentment.

We also journeyed through the pathway of 'essence', the things that matter the most. I'm sure you now see why you must deliberately invest time and energy in your relationship. Remember that when the trying and dark times of life befall us, it is relationships, family, and friends that we fall back to. And no celebration is complete without family and friends to share it with. So, just in case your gaze is fixed on your business, career – whatever it is – don't let your relationships suffer.

I also talk about intrinsic motivation – the need to find your drive within. No motivation can drive a person that is greater than fulfilment. When you put this in perspective, it will help you in making sound decisions, especially when you get to the valley of decision. Remember we talked about how intrinsic motivation allows us to make decisions we can be proud of? You see, beyond incentives, we ought to make decisions out of passion.

In the course of your journey through the pages of this book, I also laid out pragmatic steps for you to follow in order to tame your foxes. You don't want to get to the top and fall because you didn't take the time to address certain weaknesses in your life. I recommend that you read this book twice to fully grasp the wisdom in it. And please, don't drop this book and continue wallowing in your weaknesses. I also spoke about reaching out for help. No one is self-sufficient; we all need each other. This is how the universe was designed. Try to open up to someone; you will be shocked by how much help you receive.

While we journeyed in the valley of decisions, I said a prayer for you: May the universe keep you from making wrong choices. Before you make a major decision in your life, always put into consideration delayed gratification – a key pillar in making good decisions. Here, you are not moved by the now. You are like the patient dog waiting for the fattest bone; patience always has its reward.

Ernst Agyemang Yeboah's words are always fresh in my heart; he said, "If you meet the darkest moment of life, strive valiantly through it with courage and never retreat, for you shall surely meet light afterward. If you meet the muddy stream of life, swim across it with tenacity to the very end for there is a clearer stream that shall wash your dirt away afterward." Now read this concluding part slowly: "If all people reject you in the mid arduous race of life, dare to smile and move on for there are people who await you to embrace you in the end." Is that not so beautiful?

You see, life is not a fantasy; challenges will choke you, and sometimes you might find it hard to breathe. Henceforth, I want you to be gritty. Spryte Loriano said it better: "Every great story happened when someone decided not to give up."

I tell you this truth: Life will require your dogged refusal to give up.

Just in case you have it all cloudy and you don't know where to start to begin the transformation your life needs, remember we talked about climbing the shoulders of people that have gone ahead of you. The father of motion, Isaac Newton, affirmed that if he has seen further, it was by standing on the shoulders of giants. Mentorship can go a long way in clearing your mind and setting you up with the right knowledge and information. If you do not have a mentor, follow the steps in Chapter 9 of this book, please. This would go a long way in moving you a step closer to the life you want to live.

***

Before you close this book and add it to the plethora of books on your shelf, I beseech you to henceforth pay thorough attention to your life. Highlight the values you believe in and build your life around principles. Over the years, I have found that living by principles makes decision-making easier. You see, think of principles as a constitution – the book of law that guides your life. Building your life around principles helps you live a disciplined life. Susan Swann once asked a very crucial question: "Imagine if there were no accepted principles of conduct. Just everyone walking in his own way. What would happen to our way of life? To our children? How do we both learn and teach correct principles, and then use them to make our lives better?"

Imagine a country that has no constitution, no rules, no government. Exactly! What will be the order of the day? Chaos! That's the word. And this is how your life will be if you do not have a certain conduct that guides your life. I believe that many times in life, we are tempted to violate the things we stand for. Perhaps, as a favour to a friend. You know when your friends tell you to go clubbing and you are not the party type, yet you still go, because, well, friends are friends. Don't be like that anymore. Learn to draw the line; have your space. Consider your values and stick to them. I say this because violating your principles makes you light; like the fallen leaves of a tree, you will be lawless, tossed to and fro.

The other day I came across the daily workout schedule of Cristiano Ronaldo. I was in awe at the repeated number of barbell squats, burpee pull-ups, bench dips, push-ups, medicine ball tosses, hanging leg raises... the list is scary! I could attempt some of that workout practice, but I don't think I could do it at the rate he does it. Little wonder he is at the top of his game. I want you to understand that living by principles prevents you from living a mediocre life. You understand your values and you stick to them; this is the way of champions.

You have probably heard in Lupita Nyong'o's speech: "No matter where you are from, your dreams are valid." Well, that's true. But if you live your life carelessly, you will invalidate your dreams. The world knows that if wishes were horses, beggars would ride. If dreaming were enough, African countries would be free from the bondage of corruption and poverty. What I am saying is, you have to become more deliberate with your life. Watch your steps; how consistent are you with the things that matter to your life? What image do you represent to your immediate environment? Do you have any virtue you believe in and that you live by? Answer these self-reflection questions, as this will usher you into thoughtfulness and finding the pillars you would bet your life on.

Aesop, a great philosopher, once said, "He that always gives way to others will end in having no principles of his own." Unfortunately, some folks are houses without doors, open to everyone. They give room for anything and everything. They stand for nothing, and as a result, they live for nothing.

I understand that it's not easy to stay thorough to principles. Nipsey Hussle once said, "It sounds simple telling people to work hard and never quit, but to really execute and demonstrate those principles takes discipline and faith. Discipline and Faith. Those are the two factors that I believe separate the good from the great, the successes from the failures."

It's easy to set standards and priorities and still fall short of them. But you, dear reader, must not settle for a life of mediocrity; you can make the rest of your life the best of life. Brace up and live intentionally! I call you blessed.

AUTHOR'S NOTE

Thank you for the time you have taken to read this book. I hope you enjoyed the essays in it.

If you loved the book and have a minute to spare, I would appreciate a short review on the page or site where you bought it. I greatly appreciate your help in promoting my work. Reviews from readers like you make a huge difference in helping new readers choose a book.

Thank you!

Deji Ajibade

AUTHOR'S BIO

Deji Ajibade is a Nigerian-born writer. He holds a master's degree in clinical psychology from the prestigious Obafemi Awolowo University, Nigeria.

He is passionate about and dedicated to using counselling to help people navigate through everyday life issues and ensuring that they lead more productive lives.

Deji actively trades in foreign exchange in the world of finance. He's also a lover of nature and the arts.